MERLINS

of the Wicklow Mountains

MERLINS

of the Wicklow Mountains

ANTHONY MCELHERON

CURRACH
PRESS

First published in 2005 by
CURRACH PRESS
55A Spruce Avenue, Stillorgan Industrial Park, Blackrock, Co. Dublin

www.currach.ie

Cover and book design by Paul McElheron & Associates, Dublin
Editorial and index by Carole C. Devaney, Dublin
Front cover photograph by John Knight
Back cover photograph by Stephen Mills
Printed by Nørhaven Book A/S, Denmark

The author has asserted his moral rights.

ISBN 1-85607-933-3

Contents

THIS PUBLICATION WAS SPONSORED BY

AN ROINN COMHSHAOIL, OIDHREACHTA AGUS RIALTAIS ÁITIÚIL

DEPARTMENT OF THE LOCAL ENVIRONMENT, HERITAGE
AND LOCAL GOVERNMENT

AND

SUPPORTED BY THE HERITAGE COUNCIL

LE CUIDIÚ AN CHOMHAIRLE OIDHREACHTA

For Catherine and Tory

Acknowledgements

I would like to express my grateful appreciation and thanks to all those who assisted me with this publication.

My colleagues in the National Parks and Wildlife Service (NPWS) helped me in many ways. Sean Casey and Wesley Atkinson allowed me the leeway to devote the many extra hours required for study. Enda Mullen spent many hours with me at the Duff Hill site and the book gained much from her comments. Ciara Flynn, David Norriss, Lorcan Scott and Val Swan provided most useful additional information about the birds' status in other counties. Damian Clarke and Judit Kelemen contributed many suggestions for future management of the species in Co. Wicklow.

Hugh McLindon provided the beautiful drawings.

Barry Coad (Coillte Teo) supplied vital information about forestation in the county.

Mick Boyle and Padraig Farrelly were knowledgeable and humorous companions during the density study.

Laura Scanlan also spent many hours at the Duff Hill site with me and helped provide information about bird populations at adjoining sites.

The stunning photographs were produced by Helen Boland, John Knight, Frank Doyle, Mike Brown, Stephen Mills, Eamon de Buitléar, John Griffin and Lorcan Scott.

Finally my wife, Anne, typed the text, corrected the numerous misspellings and grammatical gridlocks, and suggested many ways to improve the presentation.

My sincere thanks to all of you.

Anthony McElheron
September 2005

Preface

The passing of the Wildlife Act, 1976 saw the introduction of 'Authorised Persons' under Section 72. The majority of these people were subsequently entitled 'Wildlife Rangers' and were entrusted with implementing the provisions of the Act. I was appointed in November 1979 (as it happened, I was the first). The initial years were mainly spent familiarising ourselves with our areas of operation and getting to know something of the distribution and density of protected flora and fauna, both aquatic and terrestrial.

During the early 1980s, I spent some time investigating the population of peregrine falcons with my friend, the late Jim Haine, RIP. Our journeys into remote parts of Co. Wicklow brought us into very occasional visual or audible contact with the tiny moorland falcon, the merlin. I tried to get information about the bird in the county, but soon realised that none was available. Any historical evidence was localised, sporadic and anecdotal.

In 1987, David Norriss of the National Parks and Wildlife Service initiated a research project examining habitat requirements for breeding merlin. Six areas were chosen — one in Kildare, one in Mayo and two each in Donegal and Wicklow. Areas were designated simply according to the availability of interested staff. I was involved, along with six others, in this project for five years.

On completion of this research programme, I sought and was given opportunities to continue my investigations. It was only then that patterns emerged and territorial perimeters unfolded. Note-taking began, locations, site descriptions, behavioural activities, call signs — all were recorded. An extended stay at the merlin breeding site near Duff Hill revealed activities of the species which I knew were not in the public domain.

The highly secretive merlin made investigation extremely difficult. The total absence of local or national information, or an acknowledged methodology, meant I was starting from scratch. This compelling challenge soon developed into a passion. Eventually, I felt I had accumulated enough information to consider how to develop my findings.

I am not a scientist. My formal training was at law. So the publication of a 'paper' was an option I was neither inclined towards nor felt capable of. Thus, this is a personal account of my work with merlins, based solely on close and detailed observations made at selected sites over a number of years. This labour of love, which began nearly 20 years ago, is now and forever will be one of the great passions of my life.

BACKGROUND

The reasons for the decline of the peregrine falcon population in the 1950s and '60s are well documented, as are the reasons for its subsequent recovery. That decline roughly coincided with a drop in merlin numbers in some areas, including Co. Wicklow. In most instances, the reasons attributed to the peregrine decline were the same as those proffered for the drop in the merlin population.

It must be borne in mind, however, that the amount of field work and general monitoring of the peregrine falcon far outweighed that of its much smaller, fellow moorland dweller, the merlin. It is probable that the intake of environmental contaminants contributed to the accelerated merlin decline during the non-breeding season. This may have occurred during the females' winter occupation of coastal areas. It should also be remembered that most of the intensively cultivated farmland lies in the east of Co. Wicklow. Small prey species, such as the meadow pipit, also spent the winter in these milder coastal places (like their predators, the female merlins) and probably accumulated high pesticide levels during their stay. Thinning of eggshells and consequent breaking during the early part of the breeding season were the inevitable result.

However, farming methods in Ireland during the 1950s and '60s were on a much smaller and less intensive scale than those in England and, more importantly, Wales, where the initial investigations into merlin populations were conducted. The amount of contaminants used in coastal farmland areas in Co. Wicklow was correspondingly less and in many cases non-existent. Therefore, there must have been other factors contributing to the decline of the merlin population.

For some upland sheep farmers in the county, burning heather during dry periods, in order to encourage grass growth, was a long-standing tradition. The only other burning carried out was limited grouse management patch burning. This was done under a strict and supervised regime, mainly by keepers on the larger estates. The interventions by a small number of sheep farmers, on the other hand, were exercises in the mindless destruction of vast tracts of pristine moorland. Increased lambing subsidies during the 1960s and early '70s further exacerbated the pressure for more grazing. Huge areas of mixed age heather (including well-developed, closed-canopy, single species stands) were incinerated. As the breeding habitat of its main prey species, the meadow pipit, was destroyed, so too did the traditional ground-nesting merlin lose its breeding stations. This annual destruction on an indiscriminate level continued unabated. The birds were simply burnt 'out of house and home'. In places, it would take anywhere between 8 and 20 years for the habitat to recover completely.

★ ★ ★

Up to four cream-coloured eggs with red-brown freckles are laid in a scrape on dry turf, usually with a heather overhang. Incubation, by both parents, lasts for about 30 days. The oldest documented evidence found of a ground nest in Co. Wicklow is one at Upper Lough Bray in the 1950s. The traditional ground nest of merlins is now a rarity in the county.

The dwindling numbers of breeding pairs of merlin would find a few places of relative safety to sustain the fast-declining population. Areas of mixed woodland, which had contained tree-nesting birds since records began, would prove pivotal in the species' survival. The Coronation Plantation was, and still is, one of the most reliable and safe breeding sites for the species in the county. Southern parts of the Glencree valley, bordering Maulin and Tonduff mountains, and areas bordering Co. Dublin, near Prince William's Seat Mountain, also remained safe from the annual destruction. The huge areas of land surrounding Glendalough and Glenmalure were precipitous and unsuitable for merlins to hunt their prey. An occasional pocket of gentle undulation in this mountainous area might provide a secure domicile for an isolated pair, but that would have little impact on the population as a whole.

Uncontrolled heather burning results in devastation for ground-nesting birds, especially meadow pipit and grouse. Skylark suffer less since their preferred ground-nesting sites are on wetter ground.

The enormous swaths of the greater Sally and Wicklow Gap regions were an open invitation to some farmers to continue their activities. This indiscriminate and uncontrolled burning of moorland brought annihilation for the birds. Paradoxically, it was those two areas that held the key to the merlin's recovery.

An examination of the record of forestation in Co. Wicklow shows that the general areas of the Sally and Wicklow Gaps were first planted in the 1960s and '70s. The species chosen were Douglas fir, lodgepole pine, island pine, Norway spruce and Sitka spruce. But by far the greatest number planted were Sitka spruce. It would take a further 20 years before grey crows and magpies sought breeding accommodation in these newly provided facilities. Usually, the nests were constructed at the fourth or fifth growth below the leader. The shallow bowl of the crows' nests would in due course become the preference for the merlins, over the deeper V-shaped nests of the magpies. Furthermore, trees chosen by crows had three distinctive characteristics.

Firstly, nests were usually located in trees that were slightly taller than those surrounding them. Secondly, the tree of choice was always slightly separated from the others. This 'island' characteristic made it less accessible to potential animal predators. Red squirrels, notorious egg thieves, would find it more difficult to attack since it would necessitate their travelling over open ground to reach the intended target. Doing this would jeopardise their own safety, so it simply meant that the crows' choice of nest location enhanced the possibility of the birds' own successful breeding. The third characteristic of trees favoured by crows seemed to involve colour: after the initial stages of bright-green growth in spring, some Sitka spruce trees adopt a much less colourful, grey-green aspect, making them conspicuous among stands of their fellows.

There was something else, too. Traditionally, forestation was carried out in large square or rectangular blocks. This situation eventually changed, but in the period of the merlins' decline in the 1960s and '70s that format was adhered to with precision. When small areas failed to prosper because of

The tree nest at the Inchavore Glen is situated at the sixth growth below the leader.
Note that the tree (centre of picture) is separated from those around it.

localised disease, overgrazing by deer or reasons unknown, the uniform straight line of planting was broken and left an irregular-shaped gap. It was to these locations that merlins directed their attentions. I know of only three sites in Co. Wicklow where the birds have chosen their home 'within' a conifer plantation and in each of these instances the tree is surrounded by a patch of open ground.

Whatever about the crows' preference for nest sites, I wondered was this darker aspect somehow related to the merlins' attraction to darker plucking posts? The reasons remained unexplained, but the general pattern throughout the Gap areas during the birds' recovery demonstrated that the tiny falcon was consistent in its choice of home in these darker trees. (The plain, old unattractive Sitka spruce was proving to have its very own fascinating secrets.)

★ ★ ★

There are 24 known merlin sites in upland Wicklow. The lowest is at about 350 metres above sea level; the highest, at Mall Hill, is at slightly over 500 metres. I know of a 25th site near Roundwood, which is at 220 metres. It is probable that a small number of additional sites exist in what is not regarded as typical merlin habitat. Of the 24 pairs of mountain dwellers, one site, under Cleevaun Lough, is a traditional ground nest. It simply proves my earlier point — the site does not play host to sheep and is therefore not subjected to the annual peril of incineration. A second site, near the source of the Glenmacnass River, is hidden in vegetation on top of a huge boulder; strictly speaking, I count it as another ground nest. All of the remainder are in trees. Where the plantation is coniferous, the host tree is usually a Sitka spruce. In every instance, a grey crow's old nest is used. Where the plantation is mixed, as in the Coronation Plantation, oak and Scots pine are used on a regularly rotating basis.

The figure of 24 upland sites is a net figure: within some of these sites, the birds may relocate their nest up to one kilometre away from the original position, but are still considered to be occupying the same site. If, for some reason, the female fails to return from her winter hunting grounds, sites may be defended against all comers by the male in early spring, with such jealousy and venom that the opportunity for courtship and pairing soon slips by in the short season and results in sites being occupied throughout the breeding season by single males. Of the known Wicklow sites, this has usually happened in one site per season, but during the course of study never in more than two.

THE CHILDREN OF DUFF HILL:
A CHRONOLOGY

By late March, the Duff pair of merlins had become firmly established. Their partnership was evident from their rigorous defence of the general breeding area, especially by the male, but as yet there was no indication as to final choice of home. It was still very early. Their chosen territory was the same as the two previous years, both of which had resulted in failure. Perhaps the failures of the past through immaturity or inexperience and their early aggressive defence of the site indicated a fresh determination to succeed this time. As yet the relationship was loosely defined. The food exchanges and display patterns were destined for the following weeks and months; this early process was a simple re-affirmation of last year's pairing after the female's winter absence.

Early cementing of a relationship is essential, not only to ensure the integrity of the chosen site but also to make it as uncomfortable as possible for potential avian predators to establish in the same area. Besides, the weather in the Wicklow Mountains can change dramatically in the space of a short period of time and at 450 metres occasional snow flurries are not uncommon in May.

The following days would see the birds in quiet occupation. Feeding was an individual endeavour and no attempt at anything other than companionship occurred. Soon everything would change.

At 450 metres, dawn occurs about one hour later than at sea level. The morning of 29 March was bitterly cold, with banks of white cloud broken at infrequent intervals by a constant north-easterly breeze. First light revealed a carpet of frost gripping every aspect of the dark and bleak moor. The first rays of sun from the east seemed to take an eternity to arrive but, when they came, exploded through the huge gap between Scarr and Knocknacloghoge. Spreading a thin veil of milky yellow, they raced like lightning along the carpet of dormant heather, through the great swath of *Juncus* reeds adjoining the new plantation and finally enveloping the larch, which fronted the vast forest of Sitka spruce.

After half an hour, the female flew up the curve of the river from the south, scarcely below treetop height and in silence. It appeared that, as in the previous ten days or so, she had roosted separately from her partner but within the broad area of the intended nest site. Reaching the larch, she banked sharply to her left, revealing the stunning, streaked mottled-gold of her undercarriage. A moment later, she disappeared into the crown of the largest Sitka spruce. It was set slightly back from the river's edge and to the right of a small expanse of very old heather and large boulders. It commanded a panoramic view of every aspect of the surrounding countryside, save that of the carpet of forestry to the south-west.

From the darkness of the trees came the first continuous chatter. It lasted for only three seconds, piercing the cold spring air for miles and awakening in me a passion that had been sustained through the long winter only by the expectation of this moment.

For the following two minutes, her call was unusual — a single, high-pitched shrill signal repeated at intervals of about ten seconds. Then she fell silent. After a further 15 minutes, the call began again. From her secret perch, invisible to me for the moment, the single note was repeated, but now in a much less uniform time pattern. I wondered if she was in the process of choosing a new location altogether. If so, I began to question the wisdom of that choice. In the two previous seasons, the nest, although unsuccessful, had been about 50 metres lower in altitude and almost 500 metres down the river valley. It had been relatively undisturbed by the attentions of grey crows. Now, however, she had chosen a site which was a traditional stronghold of her adversary. The tree itself followed what by now had become a norm for

During the breeding season, the female merlin is the dominant partner. Calls of instruction and demands to her partner may last for up to two minutes.

the birds in Wicklow: slightly higher than its surrounding companions, darker in colour, but on this occasion not as distant from adjoining Sitka as in most other sites.

The choice had been made. There was no sign of crows now; the only sounds emanated from their cousins, the ravens, high above in the stillness of early spring.

★ ★ ★

From the direction of the great flat bog between Gravale and Duff, the male merlin, or tiercel, flew silently down the river valley, hugging the contours at scarcely 2 metres above the ground. He glided over the old stone bridge and, fanning his tail, rose sharply to the leader of a stunted Sitka spruce. Dissatisfied with his vantage point, he moved a further 50 metres to a more dominant tree to survey his domain. With wings folded, his nape and back appeared a much darker grey than in flight. His deeply streaked breast flowed to a half neckband of stunning white.

From his perch in the bog, observation of his partner's activity had been monitored. The choice had been hers, but his new vantage point allowed direct sight of his new home. His approval was silent and after 15 minutes he slipped down the sharply descending valley and, banking to his left, headed for the vast open moorland of the Cloghoge Brook to hunt.

Most of April for me was spent checking the other potential sites. This meant that the number of visits to Duff was restricted to seven.

Site occupation during what can be a fairly inactive few weeks can be very difficult to detect, particularly at known ground nest sites. Patterns of kills and favoured plucking posts and hummocks are much less evident and this uniformity only becomes clear when the clutch has been completed. Changeable and very often windy weather can disperse feathers over a wide area, even during plucking. The remaining feathers, usually breast and scapulars, are quickly matted into hummocks by the frequent heavy showers. However, any multiplicity of kills near a potential site is usually sufficient indication that the territory has been occupied, either by a pair or as yet by a single bird.

Because of the limited suitable habitat available, new territories are a rarity in Wicklow and general site faithfulness means that the observer's task is reduced to simply determining which of the established sites is occupied. Each year, at least one breeding area is lost due to destruction of the nest by winter weather, heather burning (especially during early April) or clear felling of timber. Birds affected in this way, who are forced to relocate, even short distances, can be extremely difficult to pin down. The acquisition of a brand new home seems to impose on them a strict regime of almost total silence and quiet display, especially in the weeks immediately before clutching.

The individuality of particular partners may make the investigation of occupancy either very easy or difficult in the extreme. Weather conditions, especially visibility, play an enormous part, but birds in general have preferred methods of hunting, varying patterns of killing and stashing, and hugely

The merlins' nest on top of a huge boulder near the source of the Glenmacnass River.
It was abandoned the next season.

It took two seasons for the merlins to relocate their boulder-top nest near the Glenmacnass River to a new site in a grey crow's old nest under Tonelagee Mountain.

differing vocal input. During the cycle, merlins, particularly females, who incline towards minimum vocal courtship, can make the ascertaining of their exact location a very long voyage of discovery.

The first few days in May seemed warmer and calmer than usual. Activity around the site was more visible and vocal than previously. Preening and plucking activities took on a more regular format and the birds occupied the territory surrounding the nest site much more faithfully. Previous experience had taught me hard lessons about optimism at this most crucial stage, but the portents were hopeful and the site by now seemed secure from any obvious human, avian or animal interventions.

On the second Tuesday in the month, the temperature was an unseasonable 23°C; by the following Friday, it had plummeted to 7°C. By Saturday, four hours of stony silence caused the hope and expectation of the previous weeks to be replaced with philosophical resignation.

During the following three days, the hours spent checking the three adjoining sites revealed similar situations. At the Coronation Plantation, the freshness of kills evoked some optimism. Inchavore and Boleyhorrigan presented the bleakness of further possible failures. The annual pattern of success and failure within territorial parameters seemed to take on its annual role. Four long days of waiting saw the temperature rise slowly to a seasonal norm. Somewhere the birds must have found time to adjust to the interruption. My only choice now was to live with them and to experience with the adults the conception, formation and future nurturing of the children of Duff Hill. It was imminent.

★ ★ ★

The morning of 12 May began in the usual chilly way. Dawn was at about 5.45am and it would take another long hour of waiting before the first sounds of bird life would be heard. Almost always, the songster was a forest dweller — usually a chaffinch, followed immediately by his peers and triggering the wrens of the moor to respond, quickly awakening the pipits and in the space of three or four minutes transforming the whole site from a cold and uninviting wilderness to an oasis bursting with the promise of late spring. At this time in their cycle, some meadow pipits incline towards early morning aerial territorial proclamation. It is at their peril.

I didn't see the particular kill, but the male's triumphant screaming as he thundered from the rocky outcrop on the north-east side of Duff was the signal for the female to emerge from her roost behind the larch and adjacent to the tree which held the nest. She alighted near the top of a Sitka, most of which had been storm-damaged and was by now deep-umber in colour. It was to become her favourite perch and in the coming weeks would make observation of the activities of both birds, in the vicinity of the site, that much more accessible.

The male landed in the biggest larch directly below her. For scarcely one minute he gorged, tearing at his prey with fierce aggression and swallowing lumps of the pipit's shoulders with voracious gulps. Suddenly he abandoned his meal. Dropping at first to the base of the larch, he gave five or six rapid flaps and rose almost vertically to his inviting partner.

Spreading her wings slightly, she turned her head over her left shoulder and in receiving her partner flapped only once to maintain her balance. The three seconds of almost perfect harmony was to be the harbinger of a much more volatile relationship. It was 7.10am on the first of five days of physical bonding. No calling or food exchange had occurred and the gentle introduction of initial physical exploration, at once silent and dignified, would prove to be short-lived.

Ten minutes later the male, believing his relationship cemented, rose from his preening to attempt a second coupling. He was greeted by vigorous flapping of her wings, a ferocious and venomous vocal rejection and, to deflate his newly acquired masculine ego, a fully extended and razor-sharp right talon. Unable to understand rejection of his overtures, he vented his anger on a hapless grey crow. Passing over 500 metres away and heading north-east, the crow represented no threat but was a satisfactory target for the rejected passion of an inexperienced lover.

Without moving from the place of bonding, the female continued intermittent preening for the next 35 minutes. With the briefest of calls, the male announced his arrival from the west and highest end of the river valley,

Food stashes (in this case, a meadow pipit) are essential to sustain merlins during inclement weather when poor visibility prevents them from hunting.

his left leg trailing heavily with the weight of a meadow pipit. Instead of presenting a conciliatory gift, he rose to the top of the larch and for over a minute devoured the bird's head and upper shoulders. Then, gliding down to the end of the fencing adjoining the river, he stashed the remains of his prey in a clump of heather.

Now high above her, he circled three times and upon the call of invitation glided slowly towards her, dipping sharply and rising at the last second to almost obscure her outstretched wings and receptive posture. Again, three silent seconds later they parted and, flying to a nearby Sitka, the following 20 minutes were spent in separate preening.

It is impossible to tell with certainty how successful mating attempts are. Generally, however, the reaction of the female is probably the best indicator. Rejections of her mate's overtures, when they occur, are so obvious as to leave one in no doubt that coupling has not occurred. Moreover, it is almost always at her vocal invitation and posturing that mating does take place. To the human observer, the quiet interaction and measured behaviour of the birds immediately before and during the physical act is usually sufficient evidence of success. Birds' reactions immediately following mating can vary enormously, not only by call and behaviour but also the impact of weather and attendant interventions may cause patterns of change during the five-day cycle.

A one-hour lapse would see a third mating, similar to the previous two, but ending the first and most important day of the birds' mutual commitment.

★ ★ ★

Dawn of the following day was masked with a blanket of low cloud, shrouding the whole site with grey mist and moving very slowly south-eastwards with eerie dampness. It was fully one-and-a-half hours after first light that the nest site became visible from my observation place, about 150 metres distant.

By 7.45am, the first sounds of bird song became audible, as usual from somewhere in the carpet of Sitka. It wasn't my imagination that the previous day's explosion of sun-bathed early morning song was replaced on this murky dawn by a less-than-enthusiastic muted chatter.

At first without any sound, the pair appeared from the area of the nest site. Fifty metres into their joint attack, the male called, his rapid, high-pitched screaming an obvious warning of aggressive intent. With the female scarcely 20 metres behind and slightly lower in height, they plunged into a narrow gap between the Sitka high on the bank above the river and the larch at the river's edge.

I didn't know whether the pair of grey crows still had designs on their old breeding territory or had simply sought refuge pending clearer visibility; whatever the answer, they were chased towards the bog between Duff and Gravale with swift and brutal dispatch. In their victory the merlins were silent, flying directly back to their favourite tree adjacent to the nest site. The following ten minutes were spent preening. Their territory again secured, the first coupling of the day took place. It was 8.15am.

At about 9am, the female flew from the nest site towards the vast bog south-eastwards in the direction of Scarr Mountain. Immediately following her departure, the male made three short muffled calls and disappeared into the crown of the tree containing the nest. The female's flight direction was fast and purposeful. About one kilometre into her journey, she curved slightly to her left and alighted on one of the smallest of an outcrop of granite boulders cresting the largest hillock before the landscape dips sharply downwards towards Inchavore. Barely visible to me, she stayed motionless for about 20 minutes, hidden on three sides by the large boulders, but allowing herself uninterrupted vision of a 250 square metre plateau of mixed aged heather on the fourth side. The tiny brown speck flushed from his ground-feeding was dispatched with minimum fuss and in total silence. The path of her return was almost identical to that of her departure. Stopping on a fence-post 100 metres short of the nest and deep in a gully containing two small waterfalls, she fed

Preening removes foreign matter from the merlin's plumage and skin, and works in fresh oil from the preen gland just above the tail. Constant preening is a vital activity for all raptors.

herself casually for the next five or six minutes, then took time to preen.

Her choice of dining place seemed a little injudicious. Usually birds will choose a feeding station where minimum noise and maximum visibility legislate in favour of their own survival. Perhaps instinct had advised her that the selection of her own home had left her fairly remote from the nearest breeding peregrine territory; perhaps, on the other hand, her inexperience and immaturity would see her fall victim to the rigorous demands of survival in the demanding moorland. Her preparation completed, she summoned her mate from the nest and a second mating took place, a little over an hour after the first. By now, the union seemed less volatile and much more comfortable to both birds. A certain familiarity had replaced speculative and uncertain courtship. Their tenuous liaison now took on the air of a responsible partnership.

The female returned to the nest and would spend the following two hours in totally silent and drowsy brooding. From his favourite perch 50 metres away, the male spent a similar time, keeping a watching brief, occasionally taking a few minutes to preen his flight feathers with delicate precision.

At about midday, he allowed one brief call before departing to hunt. This time he flew east of Carrigvore and, hugging its rocky shoulder, headed for the vast expanse of the Cloghoge bog. The area had not previously been hunted that day and his successful kill after only six minutes bore witness to the unpreparedness of his quarry.

His repeated call from over half a kilometre away brought the female to the edge of one of the main branches that supported the nest. Fanning his tail and curving his wings into an arc, he decelerated in an instant and released his kill directly at his partner's waiting talons. She fed firstly from the head and then, turning her meal, tore its tail feathers before gorging lumps of breast feathers from its rigid body. The black and white of its tail, together with the pale cream-washed feathers from its breast, floated silently down to the heather carpet. The unfortunate female wheatear had probably only arrived from her winter quarters in North Africa a few days before.

★ ★ ★

As the days progressed towards summer, it was becoming more noticeable that midday signalled a much more inactive and silent hour or more for the birds of the moorland. This occurred daily, despite varying weather conditions. Bright fresh weather seemed to stimulate birds to a much more vocal display, but even in wet and overcast conditions there was ample song. Midday, however,

Tail feather of a female wheatear

saw the pipits and larks retreat to silence. This intermission did not apply to the forest-dwellers: coal tits, chaffinches and siskins continued their uninterrupted activities throughout the day, until about an hour before sunset. Later I would learn what an important role their continually visible and vocal performance would play in the lives of the young merlin family.

Her meal completed, the merlin gave three or four rapid wing flaps and glided to a perch about 20 metres from the nest. The by-now almost inaudible invitation was signalled and the waiting male responded instantly to her beckoning. It was 1.10pm. Separate preening for the next 20 minutes was followed by the male's silent departure, this time to the south-east, and her return to brooding.

Two hours later, he returned with great flourish. His right talon trailing heavily with prey, he arced with triumphant calling to present his mate with a freshly killed skylark.

After the first two days of physical union, the pattern of killing prey, preening and brooding took on a regular format. It would begin to change when the clutch was completed, but for now the emphasis was on the routine of any couple getting their house in order.

The dull, but occasionally changeable weather continued into the third day.

The chill and mist of early dawn were replaced at about 8am by broken cloud, with increased moorland and woodland bird song. Then, at last, the first chatter of the day came from the male merlin out of the rising mists of the Cloghoge Brook as he delivered his belated food offering to this mate.

The format of the first two days continued. Fresher, brighter spells of weather, which occurred every hour–and–a–half or so, triggered a significant increase in bird song and activity. Territorial display, especially by the pipits, was inevitably followed by the victorious return of the male, clutching the remains of a victim who, in his territorial proclamation and defence, had forgotten caution and forfeited his life. The pattern of mating and attempted mating seemed to regularise. The first coupling usually occurred at about 8am, when time and visibility had allowed a drowsy moorland to awaken and afforded the male the opportunity to present his mate with a token of food to cement the relationship for the coming day. Even now, the fledgling love

The name 'merlin' has no connection with the King Arthur legends. It comes from an Old French word for the species — esmerillon, meaning 'stone-falcon'.

affair was volatile enough to shatter easily and could result in the abandonment of the site. Thereafter, coupling took place at intervals of one-and-a-half to two hours. By mid-afternoon, the general activities of all birds in both the moorland and woods slowed considerably and gradually wound down until an hour before sunset, when the light disappeared behind Duff and was replaced by silence and the expectation of another still, but chilly night. Three days of waiting and watching began to seem like a long time. I wondered what difference, if any, really fine weather would make. Dawn of the fourth day would bring new surprises.

★ ★ ★

The male's ability to slip away unnoticed in the early morning mist over the previous three days was a bit mystifying. Vast banks of cloud sat on top of the surrounding hills and it was difficult to fathom his ability for safe navigation. I had, however, disregarded one of his methods of attack. Hugging the ground at no more than one metre in height, he could safely negotiate the river valley and many adjoining gullies until lower ground provided clearer visibility. This would have the added benefit of providing him with the opportunity of establishing an attack position before his quarry had begun their own day's activities. In this way, all his hunting grounds, with the exception of the Carrigvore bog which was about 150 metres higher than the nest site, were open to him from early morning.

Soon it was obvious. Secrets of the moor, shrouded in cloud and mist for three dawns, revealed their stunning mysteries. The hidden passages of the male's escape route were no longer invisible, but bursting with the myriad greens and yellows of spring. Small trees and shrubs, heathers and carpets of intricate mosaic as far as the eye could see stood witness to the kingdom of the birds of Duff Hill.

The whole community, basking in the sun, became active and vigorous a full hour earlier than in recent days. As usual, I made virtually no attempt to disguise my presence. I had, over the weeks, stayed absolutely faithful to my observation post, parked my vehicle in the same spot and worn clothes that blended with the surrounding landscape. Relief exercise to alleviate the grinding discomfort of sitting behind a telescope was always up and down the south-west side of Carrigvore, on the same by now well-trodden path. I allowed a respectful distance between my post and the nest site, ensuring at the same time sufficient proximity to hear any calling between the birds.

At this point I was convinced that the birds realised that I presented no threat. As I watched them, I have no doubt that they monitored my every movement. Once a day, I collected prey remains from the forest fire-break fronting two sides of the site and from four or five favourite fence-posts in the gully directly under the tree containing the nest. This process was carried out at about the same time every day and the patterns of activity which I tried to follow with almost military precision became as much a routine for the birds as their various processes became for me. The collection of prey remains would, I hoped, at some time in the future give some indication of which quarry species the merlins were killing in the five main hunting areas in their territory. Recording the species killed, I removed the prey remains from each plucking post, thus ensuring that duplication did not occur during the following day's collection.

Even by 7.30am, the sun was noticeably warmer than previous days and the first bonding coincided with what seemed a totally new and comfortable atmosphere on the moorland.

During the early morning hours, both birds were more visible and spent longer periods preening in the welcome change of weather. The first food exchange, at 9.35am, was marked by a slight variation in presentation. Calling from the south-east, the male perched with his prey on the largest fence-post in the gully. Leaving the nest, the female glided slowly to a small boulder about 20 metres away. Her continuous high-pitched call vibrated throughout the whole moor for just short of a minute. Responding to her instructions, the male tore furiously at the breast feathers of his victim snipe, until the raw flesh was fully exposed from the bottom of its neck to its stomach. His preparation complete, he presented his demanding partner with a fully prepared breakfast. Compared to most of their victims, a snipe is a relatively large bird, but the need for sustenance at the most important time of her cycle ensured that the female stripped her meal to the bone.

The collection of prey remains on a regular basis provides information not only on the quarry species, but also on the approximate number of birds killed at various stages in the breeding cycle.

Now replete, she consented to the persistent physical overtures of the male. Immediately upon completion, a passing magpie received the full venom of a joint attack from a pair of birds who obviously considered that aspect of their lives to be very private.

★ ★ ★

A little after 10am, the silence and composure of the site was shattered by an explosion of calling from the trees just to the right of the nest. The sitting female, calling in what seemed a frenzy, glided from the nest onto the nearest fence-post. Seconds later, the male flew up the river valley as if released from a catapult. Diving into the trees, he chased a brown bird, bigger than him, away towards Carrigvore. It was a second female merlin. I had no idea how she had got into the site in the first place, unnoticed and unchallenged. What had promised to be an exciting day now entered the realms of the extraordinary.

By now, the female had ceased calling. Her partner, flushing the interloper from the trees, ushered her almost vertically and in total silence to about 250 metres, until they became mere specks in the blue sky. Guiding her south-eastwards with more persuasion than aggression, he ushered her towards the long-established and most adjacent merlin site in the Inchavore Glen. Now visible only through the telescope, he banked gracefully and returned in the direction of Duff, leaving his unwanted guest somewhere in the early morning heat haze.

There could be only one possible explanation and two hours spent searching the Inchavore site that evening seemed to confirm my suspicions. All of the prey remains at Inchavore - and there were many - were at least two or three days old. All of them had been gently matted into their place of plucking by mist or the overnight drizzle of recent times. There was not the slightest sign of fresh blood on any of the kills and, moreover, there was an eerie silence throughout the glen. For whatever reason, the site had gone down and I could only presume that the female, in her desperation to save her season, had sought consolation in the company of her nearest neighbour.

Meanwhile the female, her nest no longer under threat, flew to the side of one of the fuller Sitka spruces in the gully. Alighting on the canopy of lush green, she spread herself to the fullest extent. Her wings stretched to their maximum 21cm on either side; she hugged her mantle against the tree until the feathers, from her scapulars to her primary coverts, could almost be counted individually. The primaries and secondaries seemed enormous compared to their presentation in flight. The sheen on her rump and tail coverts glistened in the warmth of the sun. Finally, she spread her tail with the gusto of a lady unleashing her fan. Gently she laid her head to her right-hand side and remained motionless. I thought her partner's defence of her and her eggs had elicited a posture of total compliance and surrender. I was sorely mistaken. The lady was sunbathing! There she remained for fully four minutes — a jigsaw of browns, oranges, dazzling white and delicate washes — before returning to brood. It was about 11am.

The Lough Dan site, with picture taken immediately after the bird's maiden flight.

★ ★ ★

The male's use of a huge boulder for plucking, about one kilometre away from the nest, had increased from a sporadic occurrence to an almost daily event. This was not only unusual for a merlin, but highly dangerous. Situated in an area of flattish bog, the tiny bird could be seen for long distances and the added and obvious indication of his presence on the boulder was signalled by a continuous wafting of feathers from its flat top. I had not seen a peregrine hunting that area since before the merlins took firm occupation of the site towards the end of March, but he seemed to me to be taking an unnecessary risk when safer accommodations were plentiful.

Nonetheless, it was from here that he summoned his mate at about 12.30pm.

The use of these boulders by the merlins for both plucking and preening was very dangerous. Predation of newly fledged young by peregrine falcons is not unusual, but adults are also occasionally taken.

It was to be a new departure for both birds and the establishment of a wider breeding estate.

In total silence, she flew to the corner post in the fence surrounding the newly planted Sitka spruce in the river valley. It was significantly larger than the other stakes and held rigid by three strands of bull-wire, they themselves secured tightly in the bog by posts at an angle of 45°. The flight had taken her about 400 metres from the nest and a considerable distance away from their places of previous bonding. In the brilliant sunlight, her mate left his boulder and in seconds mounted her spread-eagled body.

It was as if they were making a public statement of their relations to their student. At the time it occurred, I was not more than 60 metres away and clearly visible. The proximity of the event necessitated neither telescope nor binoculars, and the novelty of witnessing the union at such close quarters added a new mysticism to an already magic corner of 'God's country'. Although feeding and preening continued for a further six-and-a-half very vocal hours, that would prove to be the third and final coupling of the fourth day.

★ ★ ★

Meanwhile, a situation that would make the birds' life a little bit easier began to unfold. The first really warm summer's day heralded the first Hirundine migration of real consequence. Mainly swallows but interspersed with some house- and sand-martins, the visitors came in a steady trickle from the direction of the huge gorge around Lough Dan towards the gap between Gravale and Duff. Exhausted after their long flight, they would be a relatively easy challenge for a hungry merlin.

Most swallows make very long migrations. While some other summer visitors winter in inter-tropical parts, the majority of Irish breeding swallows appear to winter in the very southern regions of the African continent. Thus, for a land-based bird it is difficult to conceive of a much longer return passage. The spring return is much more purposeful and direct than the autumn movement. In their anxiety to commence the breeding cycle, many choose shortcuts over vast expanses of the North African desert and perish in high numbers hawking in pursuit of non-existent food. Even then, the final stages of migratory flight through Morocco and up the coast of western Britain and across to Ireland can be fraught with all kinds of danger.

The timing of spring migration is of the essence. If a bird arrives too early, changeable weather in April and May can make freezing or starving to death a real possibility. If arrival is too late, the availability of breeding territory and time for moulting may mean that the season has been lost altogether. The autumn return, on the other hand, is much more casual. Warm weather and ample food supply are usually available for most of September and occasionally into mid-October.

Other migrant species that are important in the diet of the merlin — chiefly wheatears — arrive much earlier, mainly in late March and throughout April. Once over land, the movement to their breeding quarters mostly consists of fairly short flights, with frequent intervals spent ground-feeding. This makes them much less susceptible to predation than the continually airborne passage of the swallow. The wheatears' earlier arrival is of paramount importance to the female merlin. The numbers of spring migrants added to the scarce pickings of the early spring moorland diet ensure that the merlin has sufficient opportunity to achieve optimum physical condition before her cycle commences.

The main passage of swallows, on the other hand, occurs during the mating process of the merlins. This ensures that a plentiful supply of tired migrants leaves the merlins with more energy to devote to the business in hand. The main northerly movement of Hirundines through the gorges around Lough Tay and Lough Dan, up the Cloghoge, heading for the gap between Duff and Gravale, and eventually down towards the plains of Kildare usually lasts for 10 or 12 days.

★ ★ ★

The fine spring weather continued into the fifth day. At a little after 7.30am, the male slipped down the valley and where the river veers right into a large area of *Juncus* flats, he banked left towards Scarr and disappeared into the morning sun. For whatever reason, his quest for food was unsuccessful. His failure to provide provoked his partner from the nest at about 8.50am. Astride her favourite perch on the storm-damaged Sitka, she faced in the direction of Scarr and called continually for two minutes until he finally arrived, trailing prey, in what seemed a very laboured flight. Releasing the pipit at her feet, he pointed his wings skyward and gracefully dipped into the river to bathe.

Just after 9am, the day's main movement of swallows began. Flying in loosely defined flocks of 20 or 30, with intervals of anything between 2 and 25 minutes between groups, they made their way north-westwards to their breeding grounds. Each day, the main passage lasted for about three hours. Swallows only become sexually mature in their second or third year. The time between their first migration south and their coming of age is usually spent in their winter quarters.

The first travellers that morning seemed to fly with great purpose; feeding only occasionally, they passed in silence, with single-minded determination. I wondered were they the young bloods, on their maiden voyage of discovery northwards, determined to establish their first relationship and lay claim to a preferred breeding territory. Two hours into the passage, the birds seemed to adopt a more casual attitude towards their journey. Calling was frequent, the flight pattern more leisurely and occasional forays in search of food more pronounced. It was to these later arrivals that the male merlin directed his attention.

By now, the female had completed her meal and returned to the nest. I had managed, for the moment, to lose sight of the male. After bathing, he preened for a while on a small rock at the river's edge. Concentrating on her activities and expecting a possible coupling, I had focused my attention in the wrong direction. It took over three-quarters of an hour of scouring the area before I detected a grey speck on top of a rocky outcrop near the highest point of the swallows' migratory journey. It was hardly coincidence that the sun was directly behind him.

Well over 100 birds passed without intervention, until the smaller and later groups arrived in casual flight towards mid-morning.

The tiny grey rocket launched himself from his lookout and, flapping furiously, descended down the high valley with breathtaking speed. Hugging the forest edge, he was almost invisible at only about half a metre above the heather tops. Just before the old stone bridge, he banked violently to the left and rose with extended talons at the undercarriage of an unsuspecting swallow. There was no chase, no opportunity to defend, no compassion. The execution was silent and clinical. In an explosion of feathers, the swallow fell like a rock to the heather carpet, attended immediately by its executioner, who spread his wings in an arc over its body and in triumph tore out its primaries and tail feathers to preclude any remote chance of escape. With one final squeeze of his right talon, he ascended almost over my head and stashed the kill in the heather on top of his newly favoured, but potentially dangerous boulder.

Aware of her partner's triumph, the female summoned him and invited the first, and much later than usual, union of the fifth day. The second execution and subsequent physical union over an hour later was almost a carbon copy of the first.

By early afternoon, migratory passage had ceased altogether. Three swallows had been dispatched by the male in about two and a half hours. One was presented to his partner prior to the second union. The two others were stashed in separate clumps of old heather on top of large boulders in the river valley, about 50 metres south-east of the nest site. There would be an ample supply of food for that day and the third coupling, at about 3pm, bore witness to a more relaxed and self-satisfied partnership.

★ ★ ★

Dawn of the sixth day was glorious, although the slight south-easterly was moving towards the west and gathering momentum. An hour-and-a-half later, the male arrived, calling from far to the east and directly out of the light

The old stone bridge

'What would the world be, once bereft of wet and of wildness?'
Gerard Manley Hopkins

of the rising sun. Trailing what looked like a pipit, his cry elicited no immediate response. Alighting on an uprooted old tree stump, he called furiously for over half a minute. Eventually, the female glided from her nest and received the half-plucked victim, which he had left at the stump's edge. After three or four gulps, she took time to digest. Thinking the intermission was an invitation to mount, the male took advantage of the wind and hovered astride her. A swipe of her fully extended right wing sent him crashing three feet to the ground. Her rejection was emphatic. His departure towards the station to await the swallows' arrival seemed almost like a hurried and scared retreat.

By 10am, the wind had freshened to about Force 6 or 7, with occasional gusts that sent the loose *Molinia* grass around the bog spiralling in hideous dances into the ice-blue sky. The first flight of seven or eight swallows battled towards the summit, keeping as low to the ground as possible and using every physical buffer in the area to escape the worst effects of the elements. This was effective enough until they crossed the old stone bridge. From there to the summit, the only relief was from the trees. This channelled the leader of the group straight into the path of the waiting male. There was no contest.

He plucked the bird on a small mound of sphagnum, where it had fallen with its chest torn open by his lightning thrust. In an apparent effort at conciliation, he returned to the tree stump, calling until the female appeared from the nest after only a few seconds. It appeared, in fact, that he had consumed most of the chest, leaving the head and shoulders remaining for his mate. Her meal lasted a casual three minutes and thereafter she preened for a further five or six, before ruffling her feathers and facing silently into the gusting wind. His three tentative steps in her direction were met with a dignified retreat of equal distance. Though measured and restrained, it was his second rebuff of the day. Her changed demeanour could mean one thing and one thing only. The clutch had been completed.

My initial instinct was to investigate immediately. However, experience over the years had taught me that, whereas abandonment of newly hatched young, even in the most difficult and threatening situations, is rare, the desertion of a newly completed clutch, even without obvious intervention, human or otherwise, is not unknown. Human temptation, on this occasion, would have to be resisted for the sake of the birds' well-being. Besides, the now gale-force wind provided a welcome excuse for escape and time for reflection on the last few weeks, plus the promise and possibilities for the future.

★ ★ ★

Site occupation by the pair had been slightly earlier than the norm in Wicklow, although patterns of separate roosting and independent feeding continued for about a fortnight before bonding. The presentation of gifts by the male to the female commenced only in the period immediately before mating. On the basis of the birds' activities in relation to flight, hunting patterns and general behaviour, I am certain it was the same pair that had failed in the previous year and possibly the same unsuccessful partnership in the year prior to that. I had lived with the pair during the period immediately before the first copulation and remained until the process was completed, five days later. Coupling took place on three occasions during each of the five days, although I am fairly certain that two further matings on the third day and one on the fourth took place immediately adjacent to or on the nest itself. In order to sustain mutual trust, I didn't move from my observation point, except for the collection of prey remains, and the nest proper was just out of my vision from that point. However, on the occasion of the three possible further couplings, the female's call of invitation was clearly audible and the male's subsequent behaviour signalled successful union.

Five principal areas of hunting had been used up to this point. The Cloghoge Brook is a vast expanse of low-lying, mainly dry areas. Large tracts of heather of various ages were interspersed with pockets of rough grass and occasional patches of *Juncus*. There was an expansive mosaic of standing and running water, and the entire area played host to a thriving population of meadow pipits.

The adjoining bog on the shoulder of Carrigvore was broken sporadically by swift-running deep rivulets. Banks of heather on their sides contained a few pairs of pipits, but wrens were more abundant. It was, however, within the context of the overall Duff territory, the stronghold of skylarks, with very occasional snipe also available.

The area towards the Inchavore Glen and leading towards Scarr was a much more mixed bag. Areas of well-dispersed heather were broken by wet patches with clumps of *Scirpus* grass. It was more rugged than Cloghoge or Carrigvore, and contained a new Sitka spruce plantation.

The gorge between Duff and Gravale was the most precipitous in the territory. During the early part of the season, it was constantly under cloud and even at the height of the season was rarely used since the steep and rocky outcrops were totally unsuitable terrain in which merlins could hunt.

The Cloghoge Brook is a huge area of well-dispersed heather of mixed age. Criss-crossed by an abundance of both standing and running water, it is ideal hunting ground for merlins.

The passage of Hirundines, even for less than a fortnight, yielded an abundant supply of easily available food at a vital stage of the cycle. Properly speaking, it was an area of temporary entrapment rather than a true hunting ground. But until the birds of the moorland began hatching, it was an essential element in the whole process.

Lastly, there was a huge carpet of Sitka spruce sprawling towards the west. Soon, its hitherto unknown contribution to the equation would unfold.

★ ★ ★

The following few days would see several changes in the merlins' behaviour patterns. After five days of almost continuous brooding, the female was anxious to explore the hunting grounds of the moor, which had, during that time, been almost the sole prerogative of her mate. On several occasions during this period, her habit was to leave the nest, ascend to her favourite perch and call continuously until the male obeyed her instruction and

Ignoring the closed-canopy stand of heather in the foreground, the female merlin flies in the direction of the more dispersed heather to hunt.

tended to the clutch. With the cessation of bonding, her vocal input, with the exception of that instruction, became minimal. This reversal of roles lasted for about three days before the duties became a shared responsibility. In fact, with the exception of the early morning territorial proclamations of all the birds in the area, the moor acquired a more restrained vocal atmosphere, as the other inhabitants, in turn, devoted their attentions to their newly completed clutches. The occasional intrusion by grey crows or magpies was greeted with ferociously aggressive counter-attacks, well before the intruder had a chance to get anywhere near the nest. The method of attack used, mainly by the male, was similar to the assaults on the undercarriage of passing swallows. Magpies seemed less able to escape the blinding speed of the tiny grey merlin and during those few days the intruders quickly learned to give the territory a very wide berth.

From then until the end of their season, the particular hunting territories chosen took on an almost rigid pattern. As the migration of Hirundines began to slow to a trickle, so the merlins' pursuit of quarry in that area slowed with it. The bog around the shoulder of Carrigvore, which was the stronghold of skylarks, was hunted less frequently than the three remaining areas. I can only presume that this was because the skylarks require a much larger breeding territory than pipits and the chances of a successful hunt were correspondingly reduced by the lower population density.

The Cloghoge Brook and Inchavore Glen, however, were raided with precise alternation. This had the simple effect of allowing the hunted time to settle and feed after an attack, but also increased the element of surprise for the hunters' subsequent endeavours in that same area. The total daily number of birds killed by the pair during the week after the completion of the clutch averaged five. Interestingly, an initial tot of quarry killed in the days immediately preceding and during bonding showed a ratio of 7:1 in favour of pipits over skylarks. The fortnight or so before that was much more difficult to assess since the prey remains were spread over a huge area in the then prospective territory and occasional tree-plucking in that wider area meant that some kills were virtually impossible to find.

★ ★ ★

Summer's eventual arrival saw the end of the swallow migration and its temporary, but vital food bounty. Alternative sources would have to be found and the huge area of Sitka spruce, the fifth and final hunting area, stood ready for harvesting by the merlins in an unexpected way.

The introduction of fire-breaks in blanket forestry was an innovation designed simply to prevent or delay the spread of fire to adjoining forest properties. Usually they were about 25 metres wide and were planned to minimise loss. Where the terrain was precipitous, they were used in a less regular fashion than on gently undulating expanses. The plantation around Duff was precipitous in places, was very irregular in shape and extended for about 5 kilometres in length. It ran from the north-east side of the mountain south-eastwards through the Inchavore Glen merlin territory and down as far as Lough Dan. At its broadest point, it was about 3 kilometres in width. Throughout that expanse, there were many fire-breaks of varying length and width, forest tracks and other barren patches.

The whole area at first glance gave the impression of a sea of unbroken trees. Closer inspection, however, revealed an enormous patchwork of irregular formations of mixed aged and conditioned timber. Some areas had failed to thrive because of poor soil, others were too wet or, in the case of a few concentrations, granite formations had allowed little chance for the newly planted trees to root. Localised disease and grazing by deer were further factors in its sometimes sporadic development. The breaks within that mosaic contained the key to the merlins' hunting efforts and the escape possibilities of their potential quarry. Areas containing very little or no vegetative cover, such as forest tracks or *Juncus* areas, seldom featured in the birds' attack pattern. On the other hand, fire-breaks containing luxurious and uninterrupted growth of heather and *Molinia*, as well as areas of rough grassland where newly planted trees had failed to prosper, were vital.

As the summer days lengthened, so the siesta taken by the moorland-dwellers

41

Close inspection of an innocuous fence-post reveals fascinating secrets. In the breeding season, fence-posts used for plucking prey remains are always in direct line of sight to the nest.

became more audibly noticeable. Weather conditions intervened to change the pattern a little, but usually at about midday the vast area of heather and bog to the east and south surrendered to quietness for a couple of hours.

This had no effect on the forest-dwellers, who continued their various pursuits in vocal display. Siskins, robins, wrens, bullfinches, many coal tits and chaffinches, by far the most numerically strong, took no respite from the heat of midday.

Even now, the merlins could ill afford to take voluntary time-off from hunting and this pressure, to sustain continuous and regular feeding, would increase greatly with the eventual arrival of voracious young. Their innovative plan of attack was bold and deadly effective.

The vastness of the forestry carpet ensured that there were hundreds of points from outside to launch an attack within. Like all hunters, the merlins had their favoured areas for killing, feeding, bathing and preening. The rocky outcrop between Duff and Gravale, which was used by the male during the swallow migration, once more became his deadly point of launch. Having attained maximum speed along the forestry edge, instead of banking at the old stone bridge, he continued in a straight line and at the last moment rose barely above the canopy of the highest stand of Sitka. Scarcely one metre above the tree tops, he wove from side to side with electrifying movement.

The chaotic explosion of birds and cacophony of distress calls from the first fire-break were ignored. Their alarm fever alerted the birds of a barren area about 100 metres beyond his assault. That extra split second allowed them enough time to attempt escape. But they, in turn, were ignored. Sixty metres further on, the birds around the second fire-break had by now had two clear, if momentary, warnings of the attack. Flying upwards would mean certain death. Down into the fire-break and across to the cover of the next stand of trees was the only other option. The timing was perfection itself. The two warnings appeared to give the birds the opportunity to escape, but their attempts to reach safety brought them into the exposed and perilous no-man's land of the second fire-break. Many chaffinches were dispatched in flight, others were stunned and spiralled to the heather surface. Their destiny was the same.

The huge area of trees and breaks meant that the merlins had hundreds of directions from which to launch attacks. Their options were virtually unlimited. It also meant that quarry species in the canopy had no time to settle, as they had in the moorland, since the attack could come from almost any direction. Throughout the season, the technique was used by both merlins to great effect, usually between midday and around 3pm. It was continuous and regular destruction for the birds of the forest. It was sheer poetry for the observer.

The entire area drifted into the tranquillity of parental brooding as May slowly turned to June. The weather so far had been very changeable and much less reliable than in the previous couple of years. When cloudless days did occur, and that was rarely, they seemed unseasonably warm. Overcast and foggy days, particularly in the first hours after dawn, were unpleasantly cold, with wafting spirals of low-lying cloud and chilly fog. A day's hunting lost because of these variations resulted in a frenzy of activity by both merlins to supplement their losses. When weather did interfere in this way, the additional birds killed by the pair during fine spells were always stashed and held in reserve for the next interruption.

I had by now a good appreciation of the numbers and species that had been killed by the pair and in order to allow them to exist as peacefully as possible in their new situation, I considered it prudent to desist from further collection of prey remains for the time being. The only other slight change in behaviour pattern was the male's extension of his area of patrol and defence against potential predators. The merest sight of any members of the crow family sent him into a frenzied and fearless assault against his adversary. It was always a direct thrust against the undercarriage of the trespasser, usually resulting in a clump of his persecutor's feathers drifting away on the breeze to oblivion. There were, however, two exceptions. The very occasional raven intrusion elicited an attack from above and the persistent passing of kestrels, who were breeding in Carrigshouk (meaning the 'Rock of the Hawk'), signalled a silent, but determined escort until clear of the territory. On reflection, kestrels were seldom seen as a threat to the merlins at any site and were simply shepherded to safety.

Tail feather of a meadow pipit

★ ★ ★

For the next week or so, I visited the site in the early morning and on my return trip from other sites in the evening. Once the presence of the pair was established and at least one call was heard on each occasion, I went on my way. That comfortable regime continued until the 11 June.

Even by 6.30am, the sun was faintly warm and combined with the fresh south-easterly to make the kind of weather I love. After almost three hours, I feared the worst. On an almost perfect day, there was neither sight nor sound of either bird. It seemed pointless just sitting at the same old observation post for any longer. There was no alternative but to break the bond of trust that had been established over the last ten weeks.

I headed directly for the tree containing the nest. The gully, which seemed quite steep from 150 metres away, was almost cavernous. At points, it dropped so precipitously that walking was impossible and sliding was the only, undignified way of descent. Understanding the male's ability to slip away down the valley on foggy mornings became much easier. Heavy, but intermittent rain during the season had left the river in

Emperor (above left) and Northern Eggar moths are a vital source of calcium in the merlins' diet, particularly for the female in eggshell formation. Since male moths only fly in sunny weather and females only fly at night, merlins have a relatively short time span in which to hunt them.

vigorous flow and the area where I had seen both birds bathing was more expansive, but less shallow than I had imagined. Directly alongside of that were two of the most often used hummocks. I waded through the waist-high heather in their direction. A few fresh breast feathers, mainly pipit, struggled to free themselves from entanglement in the heather, but that brief moment of hope failed to compare with the sight of 40 or 50 wings of freshly killed Northern Eggar moths on top of the first hummock. Interspersed with the more colourful remains of Emperor moths, they shone like a beacon in the mid-morning light. Their stunning wing patterns distracted from the certain and obvious reason for their presence directly in front of the nest site. June 11 was just about 30 days after the first bonding on that freezing morning at the end of the second week in May.

The hatch had begun and I was in the last place that I would ever have chosen.

It was too late. As I turned to leave, there was one brief shrill call from the nest. Because of the depth of the gorge, the male was totally unaware of my presence below the nest tree. In order to retain the security of her own position, the female's alarm had to be at the last second. I will never know which of us got the bigger fright. He was already dipping over the ridge and heading for the second hummock when he saw me. Scarcely 20 metres away, he spread both wings and fanned his tail. As I instinctively 'ducked', the sound of his tiny body passing almost within my reach left me in awe at the speed of his flight. By the time I looked up, he had disappeared, leaving me in a panicked retreat back to the place I should never have left.

My relief was palpable when he returned 50 minutes later with prey to the same hummock with the moth remains.

The following two days passed without a sound from either bird. As the female tended the nest, any kills brought by the male were delivered directly to a bough at the side of the nest and prepared and exchanged in silence. By late afternoon on 13 June, the female began a persistent and demanding chant. Her instructions saw her mate slip down the gully towards Scarr. There were hungry mouths to be fed.

★ ★ ★

Whereas every stage of the birds' development is important, young are at their most vulnerable after hatching. Blind and naked for the first few days, an attack from a multiplicity of crows is their greatest potential hazard and is usually fatal. So far, the ferocity of the pair's reaction against any possible intrusion had been successful defence. Red squirrels, notorious egg and chick thieves, were present at the bottom of the river valley, but over the previous two years I had not noted them in the general vicinity of where the birds had chosen to nest on this occasion. Happily, the wider area was free of mink. A parental umbrella would shield them from rain, but a freak cold spell was a constant worry. It was therefore imperative that the parents' vocal input at this stage was minimal and as little as possible was done to draw attention to the nest site. After four or five days, the chicks would be warmed by a

Young merlin are at their most vulnerable after hatching. At this stage of the cycle, parent birds keep vocal input to an absolute minimum in the area of the nest.

snow-white down with grey buffing and a small, but vital corner of their journey would have been turned.

During the next few days, the female spent at least twice as much time on the nest as the male. Occasional heavy showers of rain were immediately followed by a non-stop vocal haranguing of her mate to sustain the impetus of hunting. The instant of his departure saw her return to silence. A new pattern of food exchange was slowly emerging.

Instead of returning to the nest proper with kills, the male chose alternatively the two hummocks in the river valley below the nest or the huge and dangerous boulder one kilometre away in the bog. Arriving in silence at any one of these three destinations, he plucked the prey almost clean, often tearing the wings of his victim completely free of the body. The tail was usually removed by holding the prey with both talons and severing the sinews with one supreme physical effort. Now, his call of insistence advised his partner of the prey's exact location. His departure to provide once more saw the female fly from her brooding and silently collect the prepared meal before returning to feed her young.

Still in its 'pin', this meadow pipit victim was only 6 or 7 days old.

As yet their calls for attention were barely audible, even on the stillest day. Their parents, on the other hand, continued their mutual calls of instruction to hunt and advice of prey location. Unlike their shrill and emotive calls of bonding, they seemed to become less musical and much more passive.

★ ★ ★

The passing of time would herald a further development in the birds' fight for survival. As the birds of the moorland in turn began to hatch, the daily collection of prey remains revealed a new and fascinating secret.

The prey remains of a nest raid. The unfledged young of quarry species are fed almost exclusively to merlin young.

All feathers are made from a complex of proteins called keratin. As the feathers of a newly born bird develop, the germinal cells eventually form into a tube, which in turn becomes the rachis or feather shaft. As the covering of the rachis breaks, the new feather tuft emerges. Now the bird and the feather are said to be 'in pin'. As the 'pin' reaches its optimum length, the covering is shed and the completed feather is revealed.

Instead of hundreds of feathers of mature birds at their killing stations, I began finding the feathers of as yet unflown young. Such was the extent of this changed pattern that by 21 June, the number of unfledged kills replaced mature birds by a ratio of over 2:1. Raiding the nests of moorland birds made absolute sense for the merlins. Instead of expending vital energy on sometimes long and unsuccessful chases, their adoption of a wait-and-see policy would bring far greater dividends. Simply by waiting for a period at a vantage point, usually the leader of a Sitka, they had a commanding view of

Bare fence-posts are not used by merlin for plucking their prey. Posts covered at least partially with moss or lichen are preferred.

the surrounding moor. All that was required after that was patience. A fruitful attack on a meadow pipit's nest could yield a bounty of anything between three and five young.

Given suitable early morning weather, the parents' hunting activities now began well before 7am. The first meal of the day was always consumed by the parents, either a shared kill or the fruits of two separate hunts. It was invariably the female who managed household proceedings. Depending on which bird made the day's first hunt, her role during the following three or four hours was one of continuing instruction to her partner. Her dominance would see her partner either provide for his mate, feed the young at her command or take over duties at the nest itself. Calls of instruction could last for over one-and-a-half minutes, until the male finally succumbed.

On clear days, hunting activities in the period up to midday were frenetic. This ensured that any change in weather later on that day would not mean an interruption in the young's food supply. By the first days in July, activity was at fever pitch and I recorded some sort of food activity at least once every 20 minutes of daylight. An examination of diary notes revealed a further interesting variation. After the parents' early morning sustenance, whichever bird was tending the nest (more usually the female) would slip from the nest and fly in absolute silence to the general vicinity of the two main plucking posts in the river gorge directly below.

Her return to the nest with a laden talon was almost immediate. The vocal response of her young permeated the whole moorland — they were obviously being fed. My collection of prey remains later in the day revealed the reason for their enthusiasm. The stashes in the gorge contained the plucked remains of nest raids. There were no adult birds among them. As nature had provided moths at the time of hatching, so the moorland larder would now provide the tender and much more easily digestible fledglings for the merlin chicks. The parents, meanwhile, maintained their own independent stash on the boulder one kilometre away in the bog.

The intricate mysteries revolving around the whole avian community of the merlin site at Duff were finally beginning to make sense. Or so it seemed.

★ ★ ★

As I left my home on the coast in the pre-dawn of 4 July, what I presumed to be coastal fog appeared to thicken as I climbed towards the site. I had hoped that the slight breeze at sea level might freshen and clear the dense white carpet, but it remained opaque.

Over three hours of total silence and inactivity at the shrouded site failed to encourage optimism. Even the gully towards Scarr, which had previously provided relief for hunting in inhospitable conditions, was virtually invisible. As I reluctantly left Duff at about 11am, the sense of expectation and excitement of recent weeks seemed a little hollow.

From about 1am on the morning of 5 July, torrential rain, accompanied by gusting wind, lashed the coast for over four hours. I wondered how my

At this stage, only a couple of days away from 'branching', merlin young are at their most vociferous.
After leaving the nest, they are almost entirely dependent on their parents for up to 3 weeks.

friends 450 metres higher were coping with the storm. By dawn, the wind had failed to clear the fog and I decided that visiting the site would be better left until afternoon when hopefully the unseasonable deluge might have ensured that the site would once again have become functional.

My arrival at the site was greeted by a welcome, though still murky clearance. Visibility was initially about 300 metres, clearing in less than an hour to over twice that value. Three hours later, the decision to investigate directly was made, in spite of the knowledge of my previous injudicious venture during hatching.

I remember little of my scramble down the precipitous gorge of the river valley and on towards the tree nest itself. Years of experience and investigation leave one with a sixth sense. Nothing could have prepared me for the imminent discoveries.

★ ★ ★

One fledgling lay dead at the base of the tree. A second hung in a grotesque position about 4 metres above, its fall to earth prevented by its right wing's entanglement in the twigs.

The remaining pair were spread-eagled in the nest. I was unable to reach them as the boughs of the tree would not support me. I used a branch to dislodge the fledgling in the tree and laid both on the carpet of pine needles beneath the tree. Their golden beaks, almost fully formed, had already developed the curved upper mandible which would have sustained them through life, but they still lacked the blinding yellow of their talons. They were about two or three days away from 'branching'. At that stage, it is almost impossible to tell whether they are male or female. I remember thinking that I didn't really care.

I would never know exactly how death occurred. They could have been traumatised by the appalling weather in some way or other. But all four?

I could be certain of only one thing. They had not been predated in any way. Their skins were unflawed and there was no apparent intervention in feather development. Perhaps one of the parents had themselves been predated or had simply died. Had the female's exertions after two years of failure exacted the ultimate toll and her partner abandoned the site? Myriads of possibilities drifted into my mind. They provided neither consolation nor solution.

I had never intended an emotional journey, but months of observation had made a purely objective stance impossible. Only one thing mattered to me. The children of Duff Hill were dead.

WINTER SURVIVAL

The area known as the Murrough Wetlands is a thin coastal band stretching from south of Greystones to just north of Wicklow town. For most of its 20 kilometre length, its width is no more than 500 metres. North of Wicklow town, however, stands a brackish lagoon covering an area in excess of 30 hectares, known as The Broad Lough. The coastal band contains a myriad of habitat types, including coastal fen, heath, wet and dry grasslands, reed beds, dunes and shingle ridges. At its northern end, the habitat is dominated by salt marsh coastal channels.

The construction of the railway between Greystones and Wicklow, which was completed in 1885, necessitated the placing of a string of large concrete blocks to protect the area from coastal erosion. These are most noticeable between Kilcoole and Newcastle. Occasional flooding means that the landward side of the railway at that point cannot sustain tree growth. Small numbers of birds use the area for summer breeding, but it is in winter that this particular part of the Murrough Wetlands (known locally as The Breaches) takes on a new significance. Hundreds of Brent geese arrive from their breeding quarters in the Canadian tundra in October/November. Augmented by over 2,000 duck, small numbers of Whooper and Bewick swans, and waders by the hundreds, the whole coastal band transforms into a vibrant birdwatchers' paradise. Winter seldom visits its harsh regime on the area until after Christmas. Snow and ice drive meadow pipit and lark populations away from the moorland into the protection of valleys and warmer coastlines. The wet, but open pasture of The Breaches plays host to large flocks of starling. Along the railway embankment, colonies of thistles attract finches of many varieties. The ebbing tides in the channels expose vast tracts of mudflats, which are the feeding grounds of many small waders, particularly ringed plover and dunlin. Further to the south, the differing and varied habitats play host to many species of both wintering and resident bird. Thus, at any time during the winter, the milder coastal band holds a huge number of small birds.

★ ★ ★

As I returned from the first winter wildfowl count of the season, in the fading autumn sun of late October, the relative silence was broken by a continual, aggressive vocal dive-bombing by four rooks near the channel embankment, just north of the disused railway station at Newcastle. From deep in a cluster of fading thistles, a female merlin made a hurried escape and, flying north, soon evaded the attentions of her attackers. Her fast direct flight over the thistle tops disturbed a flock of about 30 linnets, who immediately arose almost vertically in unison and, having attained about 40 metres in height, flew in the direction of the adjoining beach. Two or three stragglers now became the focus of her attack. Instead of causing panic by attacking the main flock, she singled out a male linnet who had become detached from his fellows.

Fanning her wings and tail, she forced the linnet to alter his flight direction away from the main flock. His sudden isolation resulted in a hasty retreat back to the cover of the thistle-covered embankment. The momentary adjustment of her tail and wings had caused the merlin to lose a vital second of momentum and the opportunity for a kill had been lost. The instant of her failure caused me to reflect on a more far-reaching reason for her winter coastal presence. Her desire to seek out the easiest possible quarry during the meagre winter months was understandable and her retreat to the coast to avoid the harsh regime of the mountains was simply opportunistic.

However, during recent years the vast majority of my sightings of merlins in coastal areas during the months of October to the end of February were either females or juveniles. Very occasionally a male made an appearance, but that was the exception rather than the norm. In other coastal areas of Co. Wicklow which attract numbers of winter visitors, the experience had been the same. Similarly, in the counties north and south of Wicklow (i.e. Dublin and Wexford), the reported observations of friends and colleagues told the same story: large areas of coastal sand and mudflats in Co. Dublin (such as Rogerstown, Baldoyle and Malahide) had been visited by female merlins each year in winter, as had the North and South Sloblands of Co. Wexford.

The whole scenario posed an intriguing problem. If the females took the easier option of avoiding the worst excesses of winter, why did the males not follow suit? And if the males retained their territories during the winter months, how could they survive in the absence of their staple summer diet, the meadow pipit?

It seemed like a daunting task at first. In the normal course of winter activity, the males would have little reason to call and reveal their whereabouts. An intrusion into their territory by another male might elicit an explosion of vocal assault, but that would be very occasional, if at all, and would last for a period of several seconds at most. To conserve energy, their

The brackish lagoon of The Broad Lough, just north of Wicklow town, is used regularly by female merlins as a winter hunting ground.

flights would be largely restricted to hunting. There would be no mate to summon for feeding, no gift presentations and no vocal territorial displays. In fact, for the period of most of autumn and all of winter, silence would be almost total.

There would be no moorland nests to raid so the pattern of summer hunting would have to be replaced by an alternative. There seemed to be no obvious solution. An occasional sighting of a male or an even rarer vocal reaction to some event or other would prove nothing. There had to be a way of proving winter occupation.

At any time of year, it is an absolute rarity for a merlin to pluck its quarry on flat ground. Fence-posts, rocks (more usually smaller ones) or hummocks are the preferred stations for plucking and feeding. However, a piece of vital knowledge that had lain dormant in my mind for many months now emerged and would ultimately provide the key to a problem which at first seemed insurmountable, but whose solution was eventually simplicity itself.

For years, the birds had been speaking to me in a language which I simply did not understand. Behavioural signs, flight displays, calls and seasonal patterns of interaction were all parts of a jigsaw which, with thought, could somehow be made to make sense. The key was to find a mechanism to attract males to roughly concentrated areas where a managed study of prey remains and activity could be undertaken.

During every breeding season, pairs of birds, as a rule, quickly establish a selection of preferred plucking stations. Whether they are hummocks, rocks, boughs of trees or fence-posts, their usage is constant and makes observation and study of the birds themselves and their quarry that little bit easier. If the birds' activities in summer followed a generally consistent pattern, then I could attempt to orchestrate a situation where wintering birds would also follow a behavioural pattern.

★ ★ ★

The rocks, trees and fence-posts of the moorland had been features of the landscape for years. But hummocks could be created.

At a maximum height of not more than half a metre and covering a ground area of about half a square metre, dark in colour and with as little vegetation as possible on at least half of the surface area, such a hummock would hopefully lure the shyest predator of the moorland to easily observed and attractive dining quarters.

I initially chose two locations for the placement of the hummocks. The first was at one of the Coronation Plantation sites. A huge area of ancient mixed woodland surrounded by vast areas of rough grasses and heather, the results from this experiment would take much longer to come to fruition than my second choice of site. This was on the side of Djouce Mountain and had originally been the source of invaluable information about the method of merlins' attacks against avian threats during the breeding season. Now it was to provide a small bounty of knowledge about the males' winter activity.

I constructed the first hummock about 20 metres from a wire fence, which was the boundary of the forest plantation. It was in a fire-break, but marginally higher than the plough lines which constituted the 25-metre wide break. The hummock was opposite a very wet area where the conifers, which had been planted about 20 years earlier, had failed to prosper; many were stunted in growth, most were dead. The wet area was about two square hectares and the hummock was roughly equidistant from the thriving conifer blocks 200 metres away on either side.

The second hummock, at Djouce, was placed about 300 metres west of the last breeding season's nest location. Similar in size and shape to the first, it was built in a flat area of mixed age heather, protected on one side by a dome-shaped, elevated mound of about 100 square metres, approximately 10 metres in height.

Remembering the birds' general preference for darker coloured hummocks during the breeding season, I dug deep into the moorland to extract turf that was almost black in colour. This would, hopefully, lessen the possibility of even the slightest growth regeneration during the winter months.

Another item gleaned from the general summer behaviour of the birds influenced the location of the first hummock: it was placed in line of sight of the last-known successful nest site. Little did I realise at the time that this detail, which was based on hope rather than expectation, would prove to be its winning feature.

★ ★ ★

The most difficult part was to follow — waiting. If the site was indeed

Jagged rocks are seldom used for plucking. However, the presence of droppings is an indication of merlin activity.

occupied by a single male merlin, he would probably have, in the previous year or so, established a fairly loose, but regular regime of hunting particular areas. Experience would have taught him where the easier pickings were to be found. The open moorland, whose summer bounty was harvested to the full, was now a frozen wilderness with scarcely anything to offer by way of sustenance. It might take some time for the bird to discover the constructions introduced to lure him by human intervention and the three bitterly cold days that followed were hardly the conditions I would have welcomed. By the fourth day, the weather had broken and the next two days were unseasonably mild. It was time to throw caution to the wind.

The journey up the precipitous west side of the wood was a hurried voyage of hope. The discoveries on the first hummock, adjoining the area of wetland, however, elicited a vocal celebration from their student. The prey remains of at least two and probably three birds straddled the dark turf on two sides of the mound. The dazzling primaries and breast feathers of the siskins' remains were matted to the hummock, their bright yellow-green outstanding against the turf, but failing to hide both the upper and lower mandibles of one of the victims. The conclusion was apparent. The area of wetland contained many pools of varying sizes. Even in the depths of winter, occasional mild days resulted in hatches of flying insects. The siskins, eager to supplement their diet, took advantage of the occasional surplus. This, however, caused them to abandon the security of the dense plantation and left them exposed over the wetland as they hawked in pursuit of their quarry. For an opportunistic and hungry male merlin, the chance was too good to miss.

Careful examination of the whole hummock and surface revealed that the siskins' remains were the only species present. Subsequent visits over the following couple of months revealed a similar pattern of events — a mild spell, followed by a hatch of insects and the subsequent harvesting of between one and three siskins per visit. Usually it was just a single bird, but the regularity and predictability of the usage of the hummock, following milder intervals of weather, provided the first concrete evidence of the identity of its executioner.

Hours of hiding behind a turf hag, high on the south side of Djouce, would eventually prove the point. Unlike staking out a site during the breeding season, there would be no triumphant calls from the merlin to alert the observer. The cosiness and warmth of the spring sun was replaced by a damp,

It would take the author (pictured here) 12 months of trial and error to know where to place artificial hummocks.

bitter and penetrating north-easterly breeze. There was no opportunity for exercise. The summer distractions and duties of parental care had by mid-winter been replaced by a solitary and unaided battle for survival. The slightest human disturbance or intervention of any kind would see the tiny bird quickly disappear into the darkness of the carpet of conifers. Two seasons of observations at the same hummock, during the period from mid-November to the end of February, elicited the appearance of a male merlin, never a female or first-year bird.

The learning curve had straightened. The experiment was working.

Whereas the first hummock, by the area of wetland, had demonstrated the male's opportunism (siskins hunting insects), the second, about 300 metres from the last successful breeding site, was, over the same period of study, to provide an even greater fount of information about the male bird's staple winter diet. On the occasion of every visit, it was so covered with prey remains that I have no doubt it had become the bird's most regularly used and favoured plucking station. I can only guess that being in line of sight of the last successful nest site somehow provides the bird with a harbinger of the bonding of the next season. By far the largest number of kills were chaffinches, more usually males. Bullfinches of both sexes were occasionally present, an odd coal tit here and there, with robins, wrens and blue tits forming a lesser part of the male's winter diet.

The disparity between the numbers of male and female chaffinches was puzzling. A cursory examination of the five sites adjoining that of Djouce Mountain indicated a slight dominance of males at four of those examined, but nothing of the order of the 3:1 domination found at the Djouce plucking station. Perhaps the dazzling flashes of white on the wing bars and tail of the male chaffinch made it easier for the merlin to see in the duller winter days; on the other hand, the brightness of the colours may have presented the merlin with a threat or temptation of some kind which I simply did not understand.

The male merlin, or tiercel, is tiny. Weighing only 115 grams and measuring 27 centimetres in length, it is only slightly bigger than a blackbird.

The occasional presence of bullfinch victims was also interesting. Their practice of foraging along the edges of conifer plantations is well known, but it is more usual for them to stay faithful to the protection of the forest proper. The presence of coal tits, blue tits and robins could, however, mean only one thing: the hunting methods employed by the merlins to harvest the bounty of the conifer-dwelling birds during the breeding season was being used to similar effect to sustain the male during his winter occupation of the site.

Launching himself from one of three or four favoured vantage points in the moorland, usually about 200 metres from the forest boundary, the tiny grey rocket rose at the last second from about one metre above ground level and streaked in a straight line just above tree-top level towards his quarry. The format and technique of the attack were almost identical to those used by the merlins during the summer at the Duff Hill site. The panic of the birds in the first two of the forest rides or pathways was ignored. Executions took place in the same clinical way in the third or fourth open space available to the attacking merlin.

As the females plundered the easier bounty of sheltered valleys and coastal borders, the males slightly changed their dietary species, relied more on opportunism and good fortune, and held their territories even in the most demanding circumstances.

CHAPTER 4

MIXED WOODLANDS

By mid-February, the gentle flow of the Liffey had become a vigorous torrent. The bracken and woodrush, which provided a luxurious green cover in summer, lay dormant alongside a blanket of rotting oak leaves. The trees of the Coronation Plantation without their summer glory stood grey and stark in the biting west wind against the steel-grey sky. At first glance, it seemed that the male merlins holding territories in deciduous plantations would stand little chance of survival in this winter desert.

There was little evidence of bird life in the oak. I sat on a rock in a stand of about 30 trees and listened in vain for the slightest call or chirrup. The sight of a tree-creeper circling his way up one of the largest oaks was the first indication of life. The usual summer residents — coal tits, wrens and chaffinches — were not to be found here.

The Diamond stream, which feeds the Liffey along by the roadside, rises high on the plateau between Gravale and Duff Hill. On either side of its banks stand magnificent Scots pine with dense green crowns of stunning circular shape. Scanning with my glasses, the movement of many small birds among the cones lifted my spirits. I crossed the stream and headed through a sward of knee-high heather to a clump of about ten of the bigger trees. The tiny birds moved in small groups of six or seven from the base of each crown towards the middle and then disappeared in the top of the tree. I was in the middle of a flock of about 80 goldcrests. Their call was almost inaudible in the wind, but the stunning flash of orange on the crown of their heads was a sign that, despite the freezing day, spring held a not-too-distant promise.

The flock kept close to the abundant cover of the trees and even when they moved on, after exhausting one food supply, the nearest covering tree was only about 20 or 30 metres away. A hunting merlin could hardly use the element of surprise in these conditions and cover for even mounting an attack was at a premium.

★ ★ ★

During the next two hours, I wandered slowly through the plantation, stopping occasionally for about ten minutes, to look and listen for signs of bird life. Some of the smaller and steeper gullies contained rowan trees, their gleaming clusters of berries presenting an oasis of colour against the grey sky. I developed the feeling that I was missing something. There may not have been much food, but surely there was sufficient to provide life for some other species. The loose scattering of the Coronation Plantation trees did not provide a sufficient buffer against the icy north-east winds, but the protection afforded by big boulders, high heather and deep cleavages cut by swiftly running streams must protect a world of living creatures against the elements.

I concealed myself behind a jagged lump of granite, covered in old heather and bilberry on one side, with cold, grey naked rock on the other. It was

The Coronation Plantation is so called because it was planted in 1830, the year in which William IV was crowned king. It is the oldest known breeding site for merlins in Co. Wicklow.

fronted by a clump of brown heather, topped by the fading buds of last year's growth. This enabled me to hide myself almost totally from the cavernous gully about 50 metres in front of me. It wasn't long before a wren appeared. Its whizzing little wings carried it from one clump of heather to another. At one point it flew into the clump behind which I was hiding. A momentary rustling against the dormant buds, a flash of movement towards the ground, and he disappeared from my sight. My tiny, if momentary, companion was the harbinger of many visitors to my freezing hideout.

The merlin breeding site in Glensoulan, beyond the top of the Powerscourt Waterfall, is often frozen. Male merlin descend about 400 metres to hunt foraging chaffinches in the valley below.

The clusters of rowan berries towards the end of the gully were soon afterwards to provide a winter meal for a flock of about 60 fieldfares. Their ten-minute feast was to leave the crop of berries on two of the smaller trees almost wiped out. Theirs is an untidy way of feeding and many berries fell to the ground. After the flock had left, these would become a welcome meal for three female chaffinches.

The course of an hour's sojourn in my hideout revealed a small, but constant flow of birds through this one little valley. I tried to make a mental count of the number of similar valleys in the adjoining square kilometre. The biting wind blurred my mind, but there were surely ten or more. If each of them held even a fraction of the avian traffic of my secret place, then there was surely sufficient winter feeding to sustain both of the male merlins holding territories during the long winter.

My search for prey remains in the area of the plantation was in vain. Deciding

Only 5 kilometres from its source, the River Liffey flows by the oaks of the Coronation Plantation. The 1837 edition of the 'Gamekeepers' Record' notes 'a tiny, grey hawk in pursuit of grouse chicks' in the area.

what course to take next, I found some consolation in remembering the difficulty of finding kills even at the height of the breeding season. The long hot days spent watching the birds plucking in their favourite oaks seemed years away, when feathers floated on the heat haze for over 80 metres, some landing in the river and making the identification of quarry species impossible.

The artificial hummocks which had proved so successful in conifer plantations were simply not being used in this mixed woodland. Perhaps the answer lay in the fact that the vast hunting area behind the plantation was much flatter than any of the other sites. There was less relief for quarry species. The percentage of cutaway bog and interventions by man for many other reasons did not apply here. I headed south from the plantation in the direction of the wilderness of Glenfleugh Flats.

Immediately behind the trees lies a huge flat area, stretching for about one kilometre before the ground begins to rise. A couple of dome-shaped rocks, barely rising above the height of the low heather, which were constantly used in the breeding season, were bare.

Glenfleugh Flats, on the south side of the Coronation Plantation, is a vast mosaic of varying habitats used by merlins for all-year-round hunting.

I walked across a great swath of *Molinia*, its winter sheen of yellow almost blinding against the pale winter light. Much of the ground was frozen, the summer pools that would provide sustenance for skylarks now iced over, cracking with an eerie groan as I headed for the rising ground.

The clumps of heather, when they occurred, were larger than at other sites and would provide enough protection against the elements for small birds. Their stunning brown colour, dominant over the golden-yellow of the *Molinia*, presented a mosaic of savage beauty.

As I began to climb, the area of heather increased both in size and height. The swaths of *Molinia* were replaced by pockets of *Scirpus*, most of which were weathered down by the winter wind and rain, and where turf hags provided protection, small drifts of snow lay frozen. I recalled from previous sites that most merlins in choosing a plucking post preferred it to be protected on at least one side to prevent their own predation. Usually that protection would be a raised, dome-shaped mound of turf, perhaps about 25 square metres in size. The only similar presentation here was a much more jagged crest of shoulder, before the landscape descended dramatically into the Lugnalee Brook. From a distance, my binoculars revealed a large number of medium-sized boulders, some covered by bilberry, but others with inviting small areas of uncovered and very dark turf.

Wind and rain had ensured that any recent merlin activity would have been blown away or washed down the rocks and hidden at the base in a tangle of heather and grasses. I pulled gently at the growth around the base of the first rock which I thought might provide an initial clue. Invertebrate life never held a fascination for me, but dull would be the person who failed to marvel at the world I had just discovered. A myriad of creeping and crawling, vibrant living creatures carried on their business, impervious to an interloper in search of feathers. I carefully replaced the roof of their world and made my way upwards to below the crest of the hill, where the terrain became more gentle.

★ ★ ★

The cold wind and freezing underfoot conditions were soon forgotten when the base of a surprisingly jagged boulder revealed old primary feathers of a pipit. They were several months old and dating them became easier when further searching led me to the tail feathers of a swallow, the diamond white shapes still just discernible on the long and elegant blue spears.

From prey remains that were probably about six months old, further probing uncovered a male chaffinch, its breast feathers still caught in the heather tops. The deep burnt-yellow of the tips, caught in the cold wind, was the reason for a growing, cautious optimism — the kill was no more than a week old.

Tail feathers of a swallow

Forty metres beyond and slightly higher up, a metre-high turf hag stood just in front of a large pool of frozen water. From the top flew something that appeared from that distance to be grey and brown. Instinct replaced expectation. The experience of searching wilderness for the slightest indications of activity ensured a personal certainty that I was on the verge of discovery. The fibres on the deep-brown front and right-hand side of the hag were host to several clumps of breast feathers, their tiny grey bands fighting to escape into the freedom of the biting wind. The top of the hag was covered with a carpet of feathers. Some were dark brown with outer webs of delicate green wash, others with a granite-grey and white inner web. There were primaries and secondaries of similar colour with distinctive black bands, the tertials in their midst but lacking the band. Slightly to their right, and just on the shoulder of the hag, were several tail feathers, interspersed with coverts and matted together with fresh blood. It was the prey remains of a freshly killed wren.

I had unwittingly disturbed a bird during its meal. But that fact was lost in the knowledge that, at last, I had an indication that male merlins held their breeding territories in mixed woodland as well as in conifer plantations. The diet may be slightly different, the preferred plucking sites further from the actual nest site, the availability of quarry species dispersed over a much wider area — but the merlins were there.

Far away to my right, a muffled and high-pitched chatter revealed a tiny grey flying machine. He scythed through the air, scarcely one metre above the heather tops, at incredible speed. Reaching the head of the brook, he banked sharply to the left and, catching the full brunt of the gathering wind, disappeared into a steep ravine on the south side of Kippure.

Every love affair allows moments of emotion. In the fading light and bitter chill of a February evening in the Coronation Plantation, I allowed myself that time.

'... like an eyelid's soundless blink
The dewfall hawk comes crossing the shades to alight
Upon the wind-warped upland thorn.'
Thomas Hardy

CHAPTER 5

SOME SITE NOTES

The decision to concentrate on the Duff Hill site was made for several reasons (*see Chapter 2*). The whole area could be overlooked from an observation point that was about 50 metres higher than the tree containing the nest. It was near a road and access could be gained within a few minutes, unlike Cleevaun where getting in and out took several hours. It was off the beaten track and thus not subject to disturbance by visitors. Several hundred hours were spent at the site during the first year and supplemented to a lesser extent in the following season to verify the previous year's discoveries.

Most upland sites have their own characteristics. They vary in size, vegetative cover, natural features and, in many cases, height above sea level. The sites at Lough Dan, Inchavore Glen and Duff Hill are an exception. All three are loosely joined by interconnecting river valley systems and are access routes for migratory species. They are roughly at the same height above sea level and on two occasions during the study all three sites were occupied successfully. The Duff Hill site holds four specific hunting areas, whereas those at Lough Dan and Inchavore, like most other sites, hold three principal hunting grounds. Because of the proximity of these three interconnecting breeding areas, the respective pairs of merlins tend to show fierce territorial aggression, especially during the late March/early April period of site establishment.

In contrast, the adjoining site at Boleyhorrigan is topographically independent. It is 'self-contained', being bordered on two sides by Djouce Mountain and War Hill respectively, on the third by the forest proper and on the fourth by the huge bog stretching towards Crochan Pond. It is the largest site in the Wicklow range, being almost 8 square kilometres. About half the site is very wet and the predominant quarry species during the breeding season is skylark. A fascinating aspect of observation in this mainly flat area is

Breast feathers of a skylark

the competition between hunter and hunted. Compared to other challenges, skylarks are generally a much more difficult chase for merlins. Their speed and agility in flight can be quite stunning. Successful escapes are signalled by triumphant territorial reaffirmation of freedom. Their adversaries, on the other hand, announce their victory by equally vociferous proclamation and, unless the food bounty is immediately required, 'pick the brains' of their victims as their own reward before stashing.

A further distinctive trait of the Boleyhorrigan site is the variation in plucking habits, depending on which breeding location the merlins choose. When the eastern and slightly higher site was preferred, the distribution of prey remains was confined exclusively to the plough lines in the fire-breaks and the adjoining fence. Over three-quarters of a kilometre away, the

During most of July, it is usual to find the prey remains of moths, unfledged young and mature birds at merlin plucking stations.

alternative western site is located at the very corner of the forest, in a wet area containing mostly Sitka spruce and lodgepole pine. Here plucking is confined mainly to mounds of sphagnum moss over 150 metres out in the bog. Spread over a huge area, detecting prey remains for record purposes was always difficult.

There are four sites in the greater Wicklow Gap area. Only one, near Garryknock, is on the northern side of the road; the remaining three are at roughly equidistant intervals on the southern side. My favourite of all the Wicklow sites is the most westerly, near Corragh, mainly because it is one of the very few you can 'overlook', making observation that bit more reliable. The heather cover is sparse and irregular, but the birds have the compensation of occupying an almost 7 square kilometre territory, which is undisturbed save for the occasional echoes from the Glen of Imaal Artillery Range. Amazingly, there is another site within the exclusion zone of that range.

Not to be outdone, the pair at Manor Kilbride have established their site within a Military Light Arms Firing Range. It is probably the most marginal site in the county and successful breeding is at best sporadic. When young do hatch, their diet is supplemented by raiding a huge sand-martin colony just over the border in Co. Dublin.

★ ★ ★

The activity over an 11-hour stint on the morning of 21 June at Kilbride was typical. At that stage, the four chicks were about 8 or 9 days old. Site notes were as follows:

6.00am	Very misty. Grey crows calling.
6.07am	First pipit and chaffinch calls.
6.17am	Mist lifting. Male calls for almost two minutes — territorial proclamation?
6.22am	General bird calling.

6.24am	Persistent calling by female — for food?
6.28am	Male with first food — nearly certain it was from stash of previous day.
6.30am	Call from nest.
6.40am	First direct sunlight.
7.25am	Male circles site — continuous calling.
8.20am	Brief call from nest. Male plucks on hag under nest. Remains of prey to nest.
10.30am	Male chases four ravens. No call.
11.36am	Female to hummock under nest. Male calling from north-west with sand-martin prey.
11.58am	Female calls from nest. No response. Male silent to nest. Female to bog under Corrig Mountain.
12.20pm	Female returns. Plucks 80 metres on rough grass mound, then to nest. Leaves again.
1.18pm	Food exchange, female to male.

After taking a break of half an hour, I recorded activity, usually feeding, on average every 40 minutes until about 5.40pm. Noting nothing further that day, I left the site about one hour before sunset.

During an average year, of the 26 favoured sites in Co. Wicklow, about 15 or 16 are successfully occupied, the average brood size being 2 or 3. One year was exceptional, with 21 sites returning fledged young; in 3 of those instances, 4 young made it to the wing. The final year of study provided a very disappointing 5 successes. Some years ago, there was a total crash — not one success was recorded and I am satisfied that this was an accurate reflection of the picture. In that year, April and May were exceptionally cold and wet (on 6 May, for example, there was 5cm of snow at the Sally Gap crossroads).

But that year revealed yet another vital aspect of the merlins' lives. Moths, particularly Emperors and Northern Eggars, are an essential source of calcium during eggshell formation. They are also necessary as food intake for the young in the days immediately following hatching. Finally, they provide for the student one of the most enjoyable features of the tiny moorland-dweller's life. Newly fledged young gain their initial, faltering hunting experiences by hawking in pursuit of these elusive flickering creatures. During that particular cold and uninviting spring, moths simply did not feature on the landscape.

★ ★ ★

In neighbouring Co. Kildare, the situation is quite different. The 6 known territories there are loosely scattered in raised bog complexes. Of these, the 3 largest sites are stripped of vegetation and are being harvested commercially. Each site is fronted by a perimeter strip of about 70 metres of bog, heather and scrubby grass. The remaining 3 sites are less modified and 2 of them have dried out considerably.

Characteristically, all of the Kildare sites consist of rough pasture and degraded grassland on cutaway bog, gravitating to rich grassland and arable soil. Quarry species include sparrow and yellowhammer, which simply do not occur in the Co. Wicklow diet. Burning of the heather is less frequent and usually occurs in areas that are about to be harvested.

An interesting feature is the occasional use of grey crows' nests in birch woods. More usually, however, breeding occurs in lodgepole and Scots pine. All of the sites are in the 70-90 metre band above sea level, about 200 metres lower than the Wicklow norm.

★ ★ ★

In Co. Sligo also, the geophysical requirements for the species to prosper differ from those in Co. Wicklow. During a visit to the Ox Mountains in late May of the same year, I found considerable variations when I compared the two counties.

Lunch is interrupted

Much of the Sligo habitat was dominated by large tracts of cutaway bog and wet rough grazing. Lodgepole pine dominated the suitable merlin breeding habitat on the southern and eastern slopes. Observations of ground flora suggested that the general area was at a considerably later stage of development than Wicklow. There was strong evidence to suggest that extensive burning had occurred on an indiscriminate basis in the past. However, there was no indication of burning during recent years. The density of grey crows was significantly lower than in Wicklow and, interestingly, squirrels do not occur in the area.

Whereas in the Wicklow situation, heather is dominant over grass species as vegetative cover, the reverse is the case in the Ox Mountains. Only one occupied site, at Cabragh, contained tracts of heather generally comparable to the average site in Wicklow. Of the 5 breeding sites discovered, all were situated at least 200 metres below the Wicklow norm and the approximate spacing between nests was about twice the distance of those in Wicklow.

All this simply means that, given the enormous disparities between the general conditions in the counties of Wicklow, Kildare and Sligo, even a rough estimate of the national merlin population could be wildly inaccurate.

THE FUTURE

Merlins' ability to adapt from ground-nesting to tree-nesting in order to prosper has probably enhanced the prospects for their future well-being. Tree-nesting has meant that three of their greatest predatory threats — from mink, foxes and stoats — have been greatly reduced. However, it appears that all the traditional moorland habitat in Wicklow is now occupied to its optimum capacity.

Welcome interventions have occurred to improve the birds' possibilities of success. The State forestry company, Coillte Teo, has undertaken not to fell trees in known breeding locations during the all-important period from March to July.

The introduction of the 1976 Wildlife Act, amended and strengthened in 2000, made the destruction of vegetation on uncultivated land an offence during the drier periods of spring and summer. Close monitoring, by Conservation Rangers of the Special Protection Areas and the Wicklow Mountains National Park, has had the effect of greatly containing the annual cycle of destructive burning. Whether by accident or design, heather fires continue to be one of the birds' greatest threats.

However, Coillte Teo has plans to clearfell large areas of forestry which, upon completion of the operation, will revert to the Wicklow Mountains National Park. All of these areas are designated for merlin within the Special Protection Area of the Park proper.

The management plan in these situations provides for the maintenance of suitable strips of predominantly Sitka spruce plantation at three varying stages over a 30-year cycle. Strips will be spaced at a minimum of 800 metres from each other and will measure about 50m x 150m. One set of strips will be maintained in every 100 hectares of forestry plantation. Although we are in uncharted waters, it is hoped that the plan will provide adequate breeding accommodation for merlin within the National Park boundary.

The merlins of the Wicklow Mountains are a stable and robust population. I hope that this initial insight into their private lives will provide a starting point for future studies, from which may emerge yet more fascinating details about these intriguing birds.

'Beauty is truth, truth beauty — that is all ye know on earth,
And all ye need to know.'

John Keats

Picture credits

Artworks

Hugh McLindon provided all drawings in the book.

Photographs

Helen Boland
pages 13, 25, 28, 33, 38, 42, 49, 57, 67 and 69

Mike Brown
pages 10, 19 and 74

Eamon de Buitléar
pages 34-35

Frank Doyle
pages 47, 52 and 83

John Griffin
page 3

John Knight
Front cover and pages 2, 22, 39, 60, 64 and 80

Stephen Mills
Back cover and page 50

Lorcan Scott
page 16

Index

Merlin breeding sites, Co. Wicklow.

Map extract reproduced from *The Fir Tree Aerial Map of The Wicklow Mountains*. The full map is available from The National Park Information Office, Glendalough or **www.themapcentre.com**